an inconvenient Journey

an inconvenient Journey

bethny ricks

gatekeeper press
Where Authors are Family
Columbus, Ohio

an inconvenient journey

Published by Gatekeeper Press
2167 Stringtown Rd, Suite 109
Columbus, OH 43123-2989
www.GatekeeperPress.com

ISBN (paperback): 9781662901645
eISBN: 9781662901652

To Dr. Lynda Nyce
Dear friend, your investment was not in vain.

Author's Note

Thank you for taking the time to read about my personal journey to wholeness and healing. The book I planned on writing required a patience that lasted no longer than a month. But what I was meant to write, what you are about to read, is over twenty-four months in the making. This is not just a collection of poems but a very personal, and intimate story. The second poem was written following a traumatizing morning in August of 2017, and the last poem was written only a few months ago. As the reader you will feel the conflict, pain, and insecurity as I worked toward rebuilding myself. Seeking the woman that I thought was forever lost. But you will also feel the power of faith and God's never-ending grace.

My healing was not automatic. I repeatedly faced feelings of hopelessness, uncertainty, and fallen tears as I encouraged the broken parts of myself, and grew deeper in my faith. And each time I felt as though I had nothing left, God met me right there. Giving me the space I needed to both grieve and feel deeply. Never leaving, He stood with me in the fire.

Rarely do we choose to go through deep pain or struggle. And, at times, we desire to sprint through our valleys, giving little thought to the lessons we may drop as we rush toward the mountain top. Fortunately, I can look back now and fully understand why I could not rush this process, which at times proved to be very inconvenient.

My hope is that you find your own form of healing as you connect with my emotional twists and turns. The dips and slips. The moments when my confidence, and trust, wavered. I pray that no matter your situation, as you read my story it gives you enough fuel to keep moving forward. Repeatedly and authentically reminding you that it is okay to feel all the feelings that come with deep healing. Because for me, all the trials have helped me become the woman I am today: someone who is still standing. Confident in her imperfections, while wrapping herself in grace, and the culmination of lessons found along the way.

— b. ricks

this much i know is true

my new beginning started with a traumatic ending.

— **genesis**

it does not matter
if you saw it coming, or if you missed
all the signs

and it does not matter if you brace the fall
with all your might

when you've been dropped, or mishandled
the impact is felt

in the marrow

because at some point you trusted
enough
for your heart to be held

— **delusions of grandeur**

she sat with her back straight
words laced with humility. pure fire. and grace

she told her story, and not the sugar-coated version
of her journeys unpaved truth

for she no longer cared if the listener
found her lessons. the blessings. and the pain
worthy enough to wade through

she spoke of abuse, and
the misuse
but also those vibrant outlines of love that had
conquered time. making her anew

and as sweet honeydew melodies
wove in and out of her life's triumphant highs, and lows
God's grace was shown

subtle. omnipresent. compassionate

healing even those self-inflicted stains. and in the end
what remained
was a woman willing to share just how much courage it took
to stand

— **redwood**

it takes courage to
put yourself back together
again

to take the time, and focus in

picking up
all those broken pieces, examining them
deciding if they are worthy enough
to have life again

for it is in these moments you recognize
unless you extend yourself this moment of mercy. this grace

all of you will stay, right here
in this dry, empty place

— **untitled**

— God, please help me
see

show me all the ways that i am worthy, and
deserving. please point me, gently away from my fears
drying my salty tears, allowing me the time i need
to feel- but also heal

because i want, and i need to know
that in the midst of the clouds
and the storms, that I can still grow. and remain
completely whole

this morning i asked God
to please fix me. heal me. and show me who i am supposed to be

i boldly asked him to shower me
with warmth. sprinkle on some much-needed grace
and i waited, impatiently
soon deciding that he must have
forgotten my name

then i looked at myself
while the sun held my mirrored reflection
and all i saw was love. kindness. strength. a flicker of peace

and in this brief moment
God showed me everything he sees when
he looks directly at me

— carbon copy

it took you miles to get here. days. years and tears. do not take those chapters
lightly. pick up the lessons. hold them safely. do not rush the process. you've
never been in this moment. remember this is not your eternity. you're only passing through

it took you minutes. weeks and months to grow here. there is no turning back. no unwinding
of the clock
no redoes or undoes. stopping is not an option. when you grow faint of heart, know
there is still fight in you left. resting in your bones. waiting to be released

every choice. every decision. every relationship has led you here
right here. so take a moment, inhale and move

forward.

— **sojourner**

hey. you have every right, while you still have breath, to say
with much conviction
how you want to be treated in this life

for we all deserve love. and care

so do not apologize, or compromise
your value
and those things that force you
to embrace worthy from the inside

— ted talk

we all deserve the love given
to that of a child

with the room needed to grow, days filled
with unprompted butterfly kisses. and someone
holding tightly
to the fragile parts of our tender hearts

— **untitled**

even on the
hard days. the really rough days. when nothing
is going right, and
everything is a fight. days where you feel lost
confused, and hopeless

unable to sniff out your truth. days when
you are distant, or emotionally
mute

even on those days. the very worst days
you deserve the same love
given
on your best days

— consistency

distance is not always the final answer
when healing

sometimes, we must have the courage
to touch the roots of
our pain. going beyond the surface of the stain

plucking it out—including the shame
and calling whatever it is by its rightful name

— **therapy**

dear shame, this is a goodbye letter

i want to return all the tears
that have been carriers of unhealed pain. the empty blame. the fear
all rooted in thoughts that outline
the design of your name

i'm giving back these false lies
all those words whispered, slowly forcing me to hide behind
your unforgiving, and unrealistic disguise

i want you to take it all back.

the feelings of
powerlessness. failure. worthlessness. and humiliations stain
for today, i declare
you will no longer have space to reign

— **how to write a life changing breakup letter**

only God knows
how truly tired i am. how soft i am, and how fiercely
strong i am

— **when you are known**

- God, i am tired.

a statement made, in the form of a
whisper. between measured breaths, and
a tightened chest. your head heavily rests
in the palm of your hand. as you wait
for solutions to your circumstance

and sometimes, the only thing to be done
is feel all the feelings
until you begin to break your mind free from the torment

piece, by piece

— the rebuild

sometimes peace and rest come later. much later. but
through each transition there must remain hope. hope in
the friendships that carry you. belief that the internal
recklessness and sorrow
will fade
and when you arrive peace, joy and love will greet you
but even then, there will still be hope. right there pushing you forward

— **endure**

she looked down
at herself. remembering all it took
to get to this place

promising that on this day,
she would only utter words her soul needed
to hear. and say

so with a smile, and tears holding
the negative thoughts at bay
she wiped the fog from the mirror, and proclaimed

beautiful you are. and will forever be
equal parts cocoa butter
and grace

— **untitled**

even as your knees shake, and
the only thing you have is your faith

when you stand with bated breath, and those
knotted tears are so heavy that
invisible imprints of struggle feel safe dancing across your chest

this is when. right here. in this moment
you must turn your eyes, and chin
toward the heavens

because a storm will calm its rage
but in your waiting, remember
you are loved by the designer of love. mercy. and grace

— **tunnel vision**

i did not really appreciate
your essence. the rawness of your power

but God knows
i need you...now

— the voicemail left to your twenty-five-year-old self
that version of you who just knew, without hesitation, that you
could conquer just about anything

and then
she had to focus on only putting herself
back together again

stitching gently around
the pain, while praying to heal in a way
that left no stain

for it takes so much courage
to rebuild again. an unwavering strength
trying to remember what life felt like before
the ruin

— **the art of reconstruction**

— dear God, i am so afraid

      that conversation you have with yourself. alone. not
      in the form of tangible words, just feelings that hit
      the core of your being. so intense it repeatedly keeps you
      from yourself. and the suffocating autopilot mindset
      disrupts your progress. crippling the willingness to reach out
      for help

but you must remember. you are not
on this journey alone
that your brokenness
will always be the cornerstone
of your strength

please tell me how
to feel
these precious tears alone will not
cleanse my mind, or
accelerate the needed healing

and someone
untether the ball that finds rest in my chest
so i can freely, and openly
see myself

— **refresh**

aren't you tired yet
that's what my God gently said

and as my shoulders fell, eyes weeping. and chest
swelled
my heart whispered, yes

so he took the burdens. strain. the pain. and desires
telling me to rest

and in this moment i realized
it never really mattered that i had nothing
left. he would forever carry me in my future, and in my present

for nothing of mine is ever
too heavy

— **when love speaks**

and while, she diligently worked toward
morphing her past grief into
coco butter healing

she realized
it wasn't the journey
that brought her to her knees. but all the memories

of relinquished hopes. and dreams

all those feelings
that follow the echo of expectations
addictive beat

— the shoulda. coulda. wouldas

it was her mind that needed
to breathe

for her heart had made it safely
through the mending

— **battle fatigue**

give yourself permission
to melt right back into yourself

again. and again. and again

— **letting go**

sometimes, you must fight
for yourself. for your belief. your definition of beauty

sometimes. you must do
parts of the journey alone. in a silence coated in
eucalyptus prayers, and self-care

and occasionally. just for a moment
you will have to admit, out loud
that you, my dear
weren't built perfect

— **the resilient flower**

hey. it is absolutely okay
to admit that you are struggling today

at this very moment.

because there is a promise, that the warmth of joy
will find you in the glow of the morning

— psalms 30

keep pouring into yourself until
you find your way back. pour into yourself until
your soul overflows. remember you
are doing this for no one else, just yourself

and then love yourself

paving the way toward deep forgiveness, and healing for
all the pieces of yourself

then press on, and keep on
pouring into yourself

— **my cup runith over**

behind the smile
and the amber-dipped glow, that outlined her eyes
she retaught herself

how to breathe

and what it means to personally know worthy, even
when wrestling adversity

— **more than enough**

dear God, i need you.

— words uttered, in the shower. during your morning drive. in the doctors waiting room, or
after the appointment. while teaching a class. right before that college test. or while
you toss and turn, just trying to catch some rest. right before your feet hit the floor. as
you pick up yet another work call. And after the abuse, or right before. behind your
forced smile. while hugging your children goodbye. when salty tears fall, in private. and
every time you try to press through the challenges in this life

you should know HE hears
both me, and
you

you should only worry
when the tears stop flowing

for this is how the heart heals the words. those beliefs
we refuse to release

— **chest pains**

looking herself
directly in the eye, as the tears made their escape
she gingerly gave her heart permission
to crack itself wide open

as she swayed. and rocked. whispering
ever so softly
directly to her soul she vowed

those broken promises
would not be the end of her story

and no matter how rough the road, this journey with all
the rumblings
will lead to her complete wholeness

— **broken birds still fly**

and when i think back at
where i've been. what i have conquered

the thoughts
that no longer hold, or cradle my mind

i am brought right to my knees

with only the simplest words escaping:
thank you, God, for seeing me

— **untitled**

i left myself, on purpose
it was the only way to survive

but now i am back

picking up all the pieces of me, slowly
for this process requires patience. understanding and self-forgiveness

and though there are parts i no longer recognize,
the rediscovery
continues to be my beautiful surprise

— **bloom**

you, my dear
are not inadequate.

so be brave enough
to show
all your sharp edges. those softly wrapped
regrets, and tear woven lessons

then slowly tell me how to breathe life, right back into all the unfulfilled dreams

for your greatest strength
will forever be
the power that comes with fueling
your own self-belief

— **a conversation before the sunrise**

and when those very real nightmares, no longer
find life in your dreams

that is when you know, without question that you
are healing

— **perfect peace**

she took a trip to the wilderness
in search of the girl she thought was lost

as she returned the flames licked
her back, hissing her name

the jagged stones breaking mercilessly
under her weathered bones

she wept. but not from defeat
for this victory tasted honey sweet

it was upon leaving the wilderness
conquering demons, and facing the eye of her storm, she realized
nothing within her had ever been lost

she only needed to awaken her heart
reigniting old beliefs
fueling everything that made her completely free

— **when shackles break**

and while her pillow
still cool from a silent night, comforted by the last remnants of
her dreams

she opens her eyes to the sound
of morning birds
boldly announcing the sun's arrival

and she smiles.

for she had lost so much, and yet
she still survived

— silver lining

i want to be beautiful. i want to be beautiful. i want
to be beautiful. i want to be beautiful. i want to be
beautiful. i want to be beautiful. i want to be beautiful. i want to be beautiful

no. you want to be full

so full,
that when you see yourself
really look at yourself
deep into your soul
you see all of you, and
still feel whole

you,
you want to see beautiful

— **snow white**

— God, do you see me

beyond the masses, over the ring of prayers. do
you see the residue of my trauma. and the burdens
i unwillingly lay to bare

please tell me, that i am worthy enough
for your grace. loved enough for your forgiveness, and that i have proven myself free
enough, to be held by only you

my eternal refuge.

i want to see strength, and
worthy
when my reflection looks back at itself

and i want to feel a peace
that allows me
to readily unfold into the softness of
everlasting hope

but what i need. really need, is to believe
even in my trembling
that i am more than deserving, and more than
just enough
as my life stares back at me squarely

— **pressure tested faith**

i do not want to just leave the carnage of
my fear. pain. and desperation
laying at my feet

i also want to be free

— **the work before the harvest**

the internal shift
back to myself has been ugly

a frantic rediscovery

but this road, though broken. and honest

has been nothing more than
a freeing one

— **rearview mirrors**

as my sweaty palms shook, and the rumbling in my
stomach was only matched
by the thoughts trapped within my chest

i realized. with heavy, bated breath

that in order to heal. the only way i will ever
fully flourish
is for this forgiveness i have kept hostage
be extended, daily. and
on purpose

— **self-refinement**

we are made up of
the forgiveness we allow

— **longevity after the hurt**

i remember the exact moment
my body came to terms with what my mind
already knew

and as my eyes wept, my heart whispered

you no longer need to move
with the limp that has been suffocating you

— **when trauma leaves its surface**

do not allow
the memories. anxiety. current pain. or future
circumstances
hold your now, and your tomorrow hostage

— how thoughts can become self-care

so keep those eyes on your sunrise
and never forget, we all have stuff

because this is what it means to be human, by design

it is what makes the journey absolutely beautiful
even when the lessons are unkind

remember there is freedom found when embracing the struggle

for you were built for this point in time
and you. i promise, will be just fine

— the dandelion

there was once a time
when the only prayer i uttered, right in the midst
of despair
was that my shame would never see the sun's
majestic outline

for i feared so deeply that my perceived weakness
would find rest in the pools
of a critic's eye

but today i'm covered in a melody
ringing with healing, and the sweetest parts of
what should be

— **finish line**

hello. it's me, again. but this is not
a typical check in

i will acknowledge that we have been together
for so long, that i believed without you
there was no me

even as my world began crumbling

yes, i recall when we first met
how your essence blinded my ability to determine my self-worth. my purpose

and over time the resistance grew weak
as you reminded me of all the things i could never be

but today i have decided that
my past mistakes never determined my value, and my bright, imperfect future
was never really up to you

— another letter to my shame

i know, what it feels like
to privately carry hurt. and have brokenness know
the intimacy of my name

yes. i understand the weighty decision
of neglecting thyself
because healing from trauma requires you to face the unhealed
hidden parts of yourself

and i know, what it means to be afraid. yet still make the choice to stay

but i also know, what it means to be free
to come out of the storm covered in the outline of victory

yes i know, what relief taste like. and what
real breathing feels like, because i am writing this
from the other side

— **matters of the heart**

life soon becomes about
all the things
you see reflecting back
in the softest moments, and your darkest times

— rollercoasters

there remains
no fear in these bones, and tears
will no longer fuel tormented storms

this battle is now over

i had briefly forgotten that i've never walked
this life alone

what once held my voice captive, and crippled my soul
will now feel every ounce of
my fury. my purpose. and results of healed pain

every ingredient that makes me whole

for this is the power, and declaration
of a woman reborn

— **hell hath no fury**

if you need to see living, breathing truth walking
just look directly at me

and in that moment, i promise
you shall have all the proof needed, to fully believe
that God can transform pain
into a ministry

— **bulletproof**

God really wants to show us
just how great he is, but first we must acknowledge
his existence

— **formation**

he told me to take his hand
so i did

timidly sliding mine into his

he whispered everything my heart needed to hear, while slowly dismantling
my fears

he told me to walk beside him, yet
all of my being felt him gently guiding

so we walked, and he talked. while my soul welcomed the healing words
that melted me

at some point the blinding darkness
crept in
but even then, i still felt him. all those healing promises more than
faded memories. not just temporary

and even now
when i feel off-beat, i go back to the day Jesus stretched out his hand
and said
daughter come walk with me

— **reckless love**

the freedom, and healing was never
free or easy

for this journey required effort, and painful moments
of self-reflection

but I found beauty, and grace
in my unexpected breaking

and now in this new beginning, I am grateful for my previous
traumatic ending.

— **revelations**

Bethny Ricks is a mother of two children, based in Ohio, and is a business executive by day. When she isn't traveling, hiking or drinking copious amounts of coffee, you guessed it, she is writing. Bethny is the creative mind behind the Instagram account @myway_withwords; which focuses on faith, healing and wholeness.

CPSIA information can be obtained
at www.ICGtesting.com
Printed in the USA
BVHW040503130820
586278BV00004B/19